ORIGINAL EDITION

JOPLIN

SOLACE FOR THE PIANO

A Mexican Serenade

EDITED BY MAURICE HINSON

AN ALFRED MASTERWORK EDITION

Alfred

SCOTT JOPLIN

Solace

A Mexican Serenade

Edited by Maurice Hinson

About Ragtime

Ragtime was very popular from roughly 1890 to 1920, and by 1900 it had swept the country. Its popularity reached its height around 1910, after which it gradually waned. However, elements of ragtime survived in jazz and other forms of American and European music. During World War II a ragtime revival occurred, and in 1973 the movie *The Sting* made famous Scott Joplin's rag "The Entertainer," which sparked another revival that continues today.

"Ragtime couldn't have happened anywhere but this country," pianist Max Morath says. "It's got everything in it because America's everybody. You have this tremendous flux, and you can see it in ragtime. You have European forms, you have West Indies and Spanish influences, you have tremendous influence from Protestant church music." Other influences include folk dances, Irish jigs and polkas. It contains some of the charm, elegance and primness of late Victorian culture, plus some of the boisterousness that characterizes the folk songs and dances of frontier America. Joplin's rags were written essentially in the romantic tradition of 19th-century piano music and contain suggestions of Chopin, Liszt and Schubert. One writer has said that Joplin's rags "are the precise American equivalent, in terms of a native style of dance music, of minuets by Mozart, mazurkas by Chopin or waltzes by Brahms." [1]

With its lighthearted gaiety, ragtime encouraged people to forget about their problems and simply have fun. Its infectious, syncopated beat made it fresh sounding, and its appeal is just as strong today as it was when it first appeared. Since 1973, ragtime has reemerged in the musical consciousness.

This edition is dedicated to
Dr. Martin Jones
with admiration
and appreciation.

Maurice Hinson

About the Composer and the Music

Scott Joplin was born in Texarkana, Texas, on November 24, 1868, and died in New York City on April 1, 1917. He was the leading figure in ragtime and a man very much in tune with the times. Joplin was probably one of the best—the most professional, the most original and the most serious of all the ragtime composers. The works of Joplin include 53 pieces for piano, 10 songs, and the opera *Treemonisha*. His music has finally received its proper acclaim in American piano repertoire.

This is Joplin's only work in tango rhythm. Originally from Africa, where it was known by its tribal name *tangana*, and then by way of Cuba, this rhythm was heard as early as 1860 in the piano piece "Souvenir de la Havane" by the American composer Louis Moreau Gottschalk (1829–1869). The swooping slides in measures 21–26 must be played smoothly. Joplin indicated the pedal marks in this section. This piece represents Joplin at his best.

Source: First edition, Seminary Music Co., New York, 1909.

ISBN 0-7390-1719-5

Cover art: Valley of Mexico *(1875)*
by José María Velasco (Mexican, 1840–1912)
© Planet Art

1. H. Wiley Hitchcock, *Stereo Review* (April 1971), p. 84.

Solace

A Mexican Serenade

Very slow march time (♩ = c. 63)

Scott Joplin
(1868–1917)

*Pedal marks in measures 21-35 are Joplin's.

31
mp
35
1.
2.
mf
38
42
46

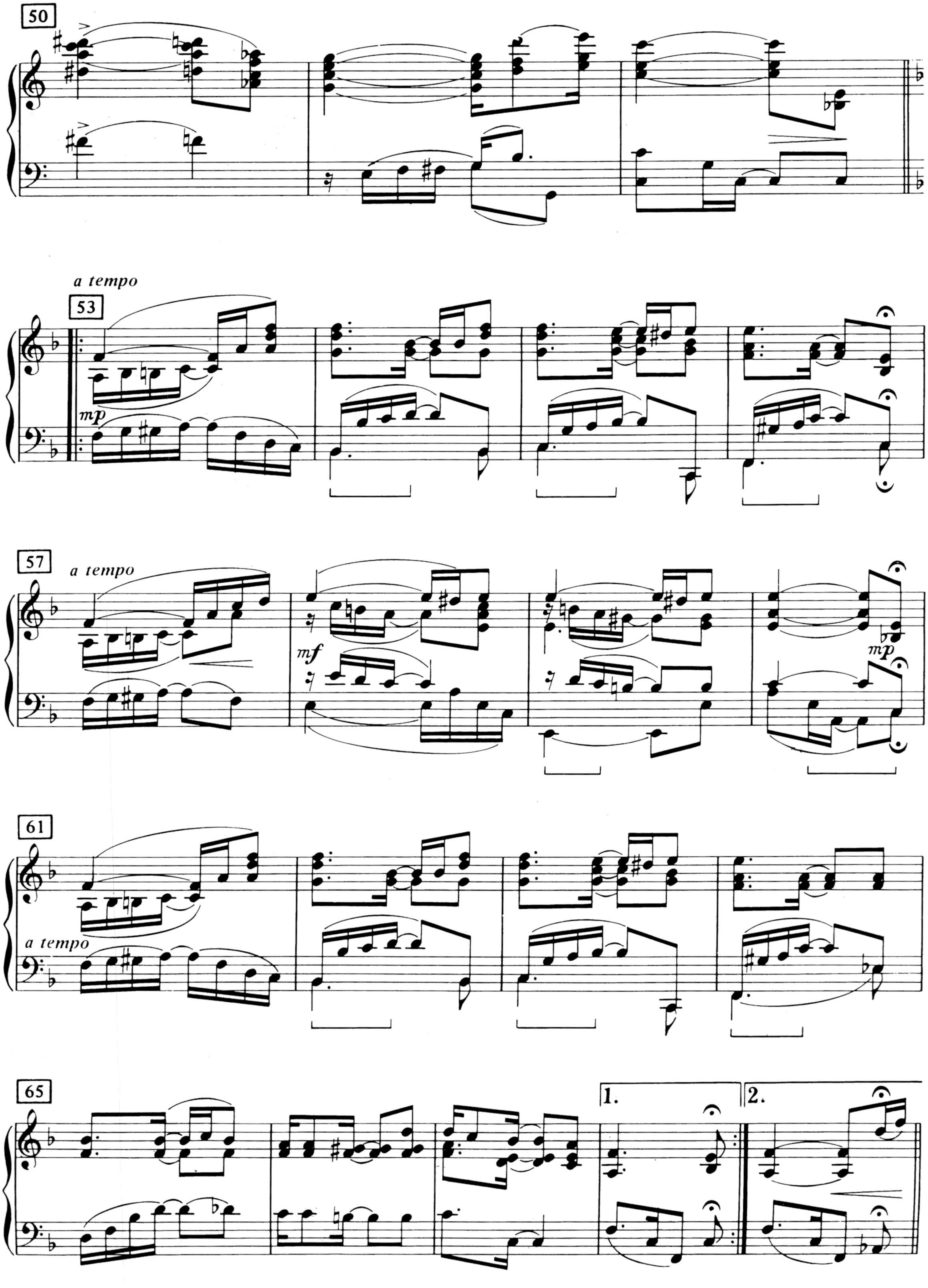
50
a tempo
53
mp
57
a tempo
mf
mp
61
a tempo
65
1.
2.

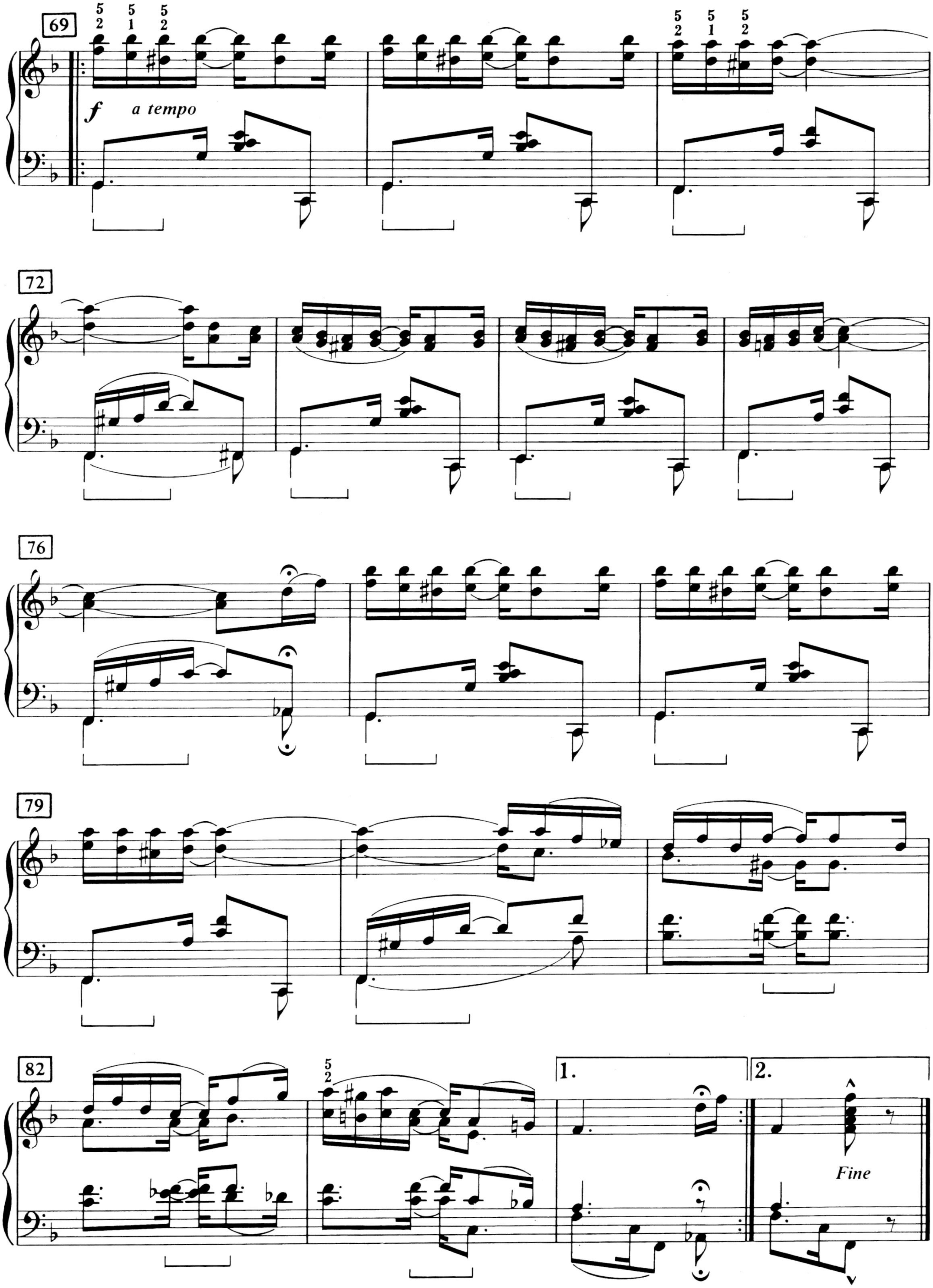
69
f
a tempo
72
76
79
82
1.
2.
Fine

ALFRED MASTERWORK LIBRARY

Most Requested

Bach/18 Short Preludes (Palmer)
Book (601)
CD (rec. K. O'Reilly) (16790)

Bach/Dances of J. S. Bach (Hinson) (600)

Bach/French Suites (Schneider) (700)

Bach/Two-Part Inventions (Palmer) (604)

Bach/Inventions and Sinfonias (Two- and Three-Part Inventions) (Palmer)
Leather (4867)
Paper (Comb-bound) (606C)
CD (rec. Lloyd-Watts) (4056)

Bach/Selections from Anna Magdalena's Notebook (Palmer)
Book (605)
CD (rec. Lloyd-Watts) (16792)

Bach/Well-Tempered Clavier, Volume 1 (Palmer) (2098C)

Beethoven/16 of His Easiest Piano Selections (383)

Beethoven/13 of His Most Popular Piano Selections (390)

Beethoven/Selected Intermediate to Early Advanced Piano Sonata Movements (Hinson)
Volume 1 (4841)
Volume 2 (4842)

Burgmüller/18 Characteristic Studies, Op. 109 (Hinson) (4829)

Burgmüller/25 Progressive Pieces, Op. 100 (Palmer)
Book (608)
CD (rec. Lloyd-Watts) (16787)

Chopin/14 of His Easiest Piano Selections (397)

Chopin/19 of His Most Popular Piano Selections (389)

Chopin/Etudes, Complete (Palmer) (2500C)

Chopin/An Introduction to His Piano Works (Palmer)
Book (635)
CD (rec. Lloyd-Watts) (4013)

Chopin/Mazurkas (Palmer) (2481)

Chopin/Nocturnes (Palmer) (2482C)

Chopin/Polonaises, Complete (Palmer) (2480C)

Chopin/Preludes (Palmer) (610)

Chopin/Selected Favorites (Palmer) (611)

Chopin/Waltzes (Palmer) (2483)

Clementi/Six Sonatinas, Op. 36 (Palmer)
Book (609)
CD (rec. K. O'Reilly) (16771)

Czerny/30 New Studies in Technique, Op. 849 (Palmer) (591)

Czerny/Practical Method for Beginners on the Piano, Op. 599, Complete (Palmer) (596)

Czerny/The Art of Finger Dexterity, Op. 740, Complete (Palmer) (595C)

Czerny/The School of Velocity, Op. 299 (Palmer)
Book 1 (613)
Complete (612)

Czerny/The Young Pianist, Op. 823, Complete (Palmer) (590)

Czerny/Selected Piano Studies, Volume 1 (Germer/Palmer) (597)

Debussy/Children's Corner Suite (Hinson) (667)

Debussy/Preludes, Book 1 (Hinson) (2594)

Debussy/Preludes, Book 2 (Hinson) (2598)

Debussy/Selected Favorites (Olson) (2495)

Hanon/The Virtuoso Pianist (Small)
Book 1 (617)
Book 2 (682)
Complete Edition (616C)
GM Disk, Book 1 (arr. Wren) (5715)

Hanon/Junior Hanon (Small) (518)

Köhler/Sonatina Album (Small)
Book (1710C)
Two CDs (rec. K. O'Reilly) (3997)

Kuhlau/Nine Sonatinas, Opp. 20 and 55 for the Piano (Palmer) (4889)

Mendelssohn/Songs without Words, Complete (Hinson) (4860C)

Mozart/14 of His Easiest Pieces (384)

Mozart/21 of His Most Popular Pieces (Palmer) (391)

Mozart/Selected Intermediate to Early Advanced Piano Sonata Movements (Hinson) (4884)

Mozart/Six "Viennese" Sonatinas (Palmer) (1707)

Rachmaninoff/10 Preludes, Op. 23 (Baylor) (515)

Rachmaninoff/13 Preludes, Op. 32 (Baylor) (655)

Rachmaninoff/Selected Works (Baylor) (2423)

Satie/Gymnopédies and Gnossiennes (Baylor) (2501)

Schmitt/Preparatory Exercises, Op. 16 (Palmer) (1709)

Schubert/Impromptus, Op. 90 (Baylor) (544)

Schumann/Album for the Young, Op. 68 (Palmer)
Book (620)
Two CDs (rec. K. O'Reilly) (16796)

Schumann/Scenes from Childhood, Op. 15 (Palmer)
Book (632)
CD (rec. Lloyd-Watts) (16794)

Streabbog/12 Melodious Pieces, Book 1, Op. 63 (Palmer) (621)

Tchaikovsky/The Nutcracker Suite, Op. 71a (Hinson)
Duet, 1 Piano/4 Hands (4858)
Solo Piano (4856)
CD (rec. Reed/Reed) (16774)

Tchaikovsky/The Seasons, Op. 37b (Hinson) (4826)

Tchaikovsky/Album for the Young, Op. 39 (Novik) (485)

Tcherepnin/Bagatelles, Op. 5 (Olson) (551)

Joplin • Solace • Hinson

Alfred

ISBN 0739017195

9 780739 017197

Alfred Publishing Co., Inc.
16320 Roscoe Blvd., Suite 100
P.O. Box 10003
Van Nuys, CA 91410-0003
alfred.com